MW01449644

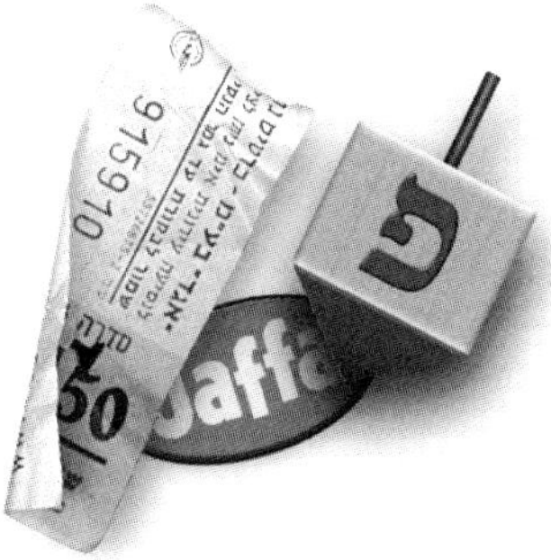

ON BUS DRIVERS DREIDELS and ORANGE JUICE

LIFE IN ISRAEL — IT'S MORE THAN YOU BARGAINED FOR!

TZVIA EHRLICH-KLEIN

FELDHEIM PUBLISHERS
JERUSALEM • NEW YORK

> *The author will be very happy to receive readers' personal stories about the beauty of life in Israel. They can be sent to:*
>
> *Tzvia Ehrlich-Klein*
> *Arzei HaBirah 49, Apt. 32*
> *Jerusalem, Israel*

First Published 1999

Copyright © 1999 by Tzvia Ehrlich-Klein

ISBN 1-58330-371-5

All rights reserved.
No part of this publication may be translated, reproduced, stored in a retrieval system or transmitted, in any form or by any means, electronic, mechanical, photocopying, recording, or otherwise, without permission in writing from the publishers.

FELDHEIM PUBLISHERS
POB 35002 / Jerusalem, Israel

200 Airport Executive Park
Nanuet, NY 10954

Printed in Israel

SPONSORS

To my dear wife Shu:

Thank you for always being there for me when life has given us "more than we bargained for."

Love, Yogi

In memory of
Meir (Maurice) Yehuda Garson z"l
and
Chaya (Charlotte) Leah Winnecour Nayfach Garson z"l:
Parents whose love for their children was equaled only by their love for their People, the Land of Israel, and HaShem.
May all who read this book be blessed with the passion and emunah to see their dreams and prayers become reality.

Tehilla

Tehilla, founded in 5742 [1982], is a non-political, worldwide movement with active branches in Israel, the United States, Canada, South Africa, England, and France. Dedicated to inspiring and educating the Jewish community as to the importance of living in Israel, **Tehilla** has actively provided assistance to thousands of families making aliyah.

Tehilla: offering concrete, practical guidance, both before and after aliyah, in employment, housing, community, and personal/family absorption.

Tehilla: helping to make the dream of aliyah a reality.

Tehilla: proving time and time again that aliyah does not have to be a lonely process.

Tehilla: recipient of the Knesset Speaker's Prize for Excellence in the areas of aliyah, absorption, and prevention of emigration.

Contact **Tehilla**:

Tel Aviv: 86 Ben Yehuda Street
   Tel Aviv, Israel
   Tel. (3) 523-2713; Fax (3) 527-9828;
   tehilla@netvision.net.il
   www.tehilla.com
Jerusalem: 54 King George Street
   Jerusalem, Israel
   Tel. (2) 625-8802; Fax (2) 624-7370
New York: 633 Third Avene
   New York, New York, U.S.A.
   Tel. (212)339-6055; Fax (212)318-6145;
   tehilla@idt.net
London: Balfour House, 741 North High Road
   North Finchley, London, England
   Tel. (181)446-1477; Fax (181)446-4419
Paris: Dor Hemschech, 140 Bd.
   Maisherbes, Paris, France
   Tel. (331)405-40110; Fax (331)476-39881
Johannesburg: Zionist Federation
   2 Elray Street
   Raedene, Johannesburg, South Africa
   Tel. (11) 485-1020; Fax (11) 640-1325

Acknowledgments

Heartfelt appreciation and deepest gratitude to:

Ron Allswang and the Tehilla Organization for the work that they do helping Jews return to our Land, for the commitment and excitement they bring to their endeavors, and for allowing me to help people see the beauty of living here in Israel;

Mr. Yaakov Feldheim for recognizing the importance of encouraging people to see the greatness of life, and of living, in the Land of Israel, and for his willingness to do something about it;

Sarah Kern, for her help, advice, and kindness, all far beyond the call of duty;

Sara Webber for her constant encouragement and many stories;

My father, Cantor Lawrence Ehrlich, who gave me the love, direction, and strength which made me able to leave 'everything' behind and come to Eretz Yisrael, and who created within me the sensitivity and inner joy which enabled me to see and appreciate the wondrous beauty that abounds here both in the People and in the Land of Israel;

and, of course, to

HaShem, Who made, and makes, **everything** happen.

Contents

Part I: Getting There

By Bus...
Now, That's Service, 16
The Pintele Yid, 19
You Are Late, 23
All Year Long, 26
It's the Simple Deeds, 29
"Street Behavior", 31
Where's Mine?, 35
Do You Have Change?, 37
It's Only Fair, 40
Time for Minchah, 46

By Cab...
The Palace Entrance, 49
Wishing You More, 52
What an Apology, 54

Normal Crazy Day, 57
You Never Know, 61

Part II: Being There

Daily Life...
　"Gut Yom Tov", 66
　Again and Again, 68
　Help on the Street, 71
　It's Nice To Hear, 74
　Mind Your Own Business, 77
　Mazal Tov!, 80
　You Can Cross Now, 82
　Time To Daven, 84
　All in a Day's Work, 87
　Doing It Right, 90
　Hope You Don't Mind, 92

Shopping...
　Morning Shopping Spree, 95
　Upon the Doorpost, 98
　Chanukah in the Air, 101
　And at Purim..., 104
　Need a Ride?, 107

No Sales Pitch, 110
As Passover Approaches, 113
Our Missing Soldier, 116
No Big Deal, 119
What Can You Say?, 123

Part 1:
Getting There

BY BUS...

Now, That's Service

It's all a matter of keeping your eyes open.

After twenty-five years of living in Israel, the unbelievable stories that are constantly taking place here still never cease to amaze me.

I guess that's part of the miracle of the Jews' return to our Land... the unreal becoming natural.

One such unnatural, natural story happened last week....

My friend Faigy E. travels to work each day by bus: it's about a forty-five minute ride from her home. During rush hour the bus is always stuffed with peo-

NOW, THAT'S SERVICE

ple in a hurry — and the traffic on the streets is awesome.

Yesterday morning, a very, *very* old man wobbled up to the bus. The harried bus driver waited patiently for him to climb up the steps one by one, and the first seat was quickly vacated so that the old man could sit down.

When he was settled, the bus driver quickly closed the doors, and zoomed away.

Faigy was sitting close by, and overheard the very old man explain to the bus driver that he had to go to the local clinic for some tests. He asked the bus driver to tell him where to get off in order to get to the clinic.

Now, this clinic is not located on the main street where the bus line runs. In fact, it is two blocks off to the right of the main street.

Faigy was wondering how long it would take that poor old man to walk those two long blocks, when the bus driver stopped at a red light.

Turning around in his seat to face all the passengers on his crowded bus, he called out, "Does anyone have an objection if I drive this man to the clinic?"

No one objected.

And so the entire Egged bus, stuffed full of passengers all rushing to get to their jobs on time, left the regular bus route. And, two blocks later, the doors opened to let out the little old man — at the clinic entrance.

What a country!

The Pintele Yid

Our cousin Charmine S. made aliyah just a year or two ago. She and her husband are constantly exploring Eretz Yisrael with their six children — and they are constantly amazed by the beauty of the Land and the people.

But in Israel you don't have to travel far to see and hear beautiful things, as she is constantly finding out.

A few months ago, Charmine's neighbor was riding the bus home to Har Nof from a quick shopping trip in downtown Jerusalem. It was a Friday, so everyone was hurrying home to get ready for Shabbat. It was also a cold winter day, so all the windows in the bus were closed.

At each bus stop, people piled into the bus loaded down with their Friday-purchased packages, shaking off the winter-wet from their coats as they paid their bus-fare.

Suddenly an unbelievably delicious aroma permeated the entire bus (remember — all the windows were closed because of the weather). A man had boarded the bus carrying bags of fresh challahs, cinnamon cakes, and *rogelach* — obviously purchased minutes earlier from the main Angel's Bakery which was located nearby.

That *delicious* fresh-bread smell reached into every part of the bus, and all of the passengers looked up to see the source.

Charmine's neighbor was sitting fairly close to the bus driver, so she had a perfect view of everything that happened.

THE PINTELE YID

"How come you don't offer me anything from there?" joked the bus driver as he punched the man's bus ticket. "It sure smells good."

The man put down his packages of fresh bakery products, took a yarmulke out of his pocket, and gave it to the bus driver.

He then bent down, took out two *rogelach*, handed them to the bus driver, and made a *brachah* with the driver.

Yes, the seemingly not religious bus driver made a *brachah* before eating the *rogelach*.

And yes, the not religious Israeli bus driver put on a yarmulke that he was given in order to make the *brachah*.

And yes, the man with the bakery packages got the phenomenal *mitzvot* of:

1) *chesed* — giving a (perhaps hungry) fellow Jew food,

2) encouraging a fellow Jew to make a *brachah*, and

3) *kiddush HaShem* — sanctifying HaShem's Name (the entire bus-load of

people witnessed all this).

But can you imagine the strength of that bus driver? That brawny, seemingly not religious bus driver, knowing that a bus-full of people were looking straight at him — he put a yarmulke on his head before reciting the *brachah*.

Unbelievable. What a country. And what a People.

P.S. And what a regular Friday, nothing-special-planned, bus ride that religious man with his bakery packages got!!

You Are Late

There was a period of several months when our friend Tova B. had to take a very early #16 bus every morning. The bus was so early, in fact, that she was on it even before the school children or office workers started traveling.

Since Tova lives fairly close to the first stop of the bus, and since there aren't too many passengers at such an early hour, she soon noticed that the same passengers got on the bus each morning at the same time. And, since the bus driver was also the same each morning, they all seemed to know the driver quite well. Many of these early-bird passengers were elderly.

Each one got on the bus and said "Good morning" to the bus driver, and then sat in his or her seat on the almost empty bus.

Again, it didn't take Tova too long to realize that each early morning passenger seemed to have his or her own, special, *kavua* [reserved] seat.

And, each morning, a heated discussion would develop between these older passengers and the bus driver — on any number of different topics.

One morning, as Tova sat watching and listening, she noticed that the bus driver was pulling away *very* slowly from the bus stop. And, as she wondered what was going on, she noticed an elderly man leaving his house and slowly making his way down to the sidewalk.

Obviously, the man didn't see the bus, because he just kept slowly walking along, in the direction of the bus stop. Meanwhile, the bus screeched to a complete halt.

The bus driver began loudly honking his horn, but the man didn't look up. So the bus driver started waving his arm outside of the window, while continuing to honk loudly.

Finally, the elderly man looked up and saw the bus. The bus driver opened his doors — which is against the law since he was no longer at the bus stop — and *waited* for his passenger to slowly walk over to the waiting bus, and climb on.

When the old man was finally aboard and paying his fare, the driver gently said, "You're late. You almost missed the bus." And the elderly gentleman made his way, carefully, to his usual, *kavua* seat.

All Year Long

The effects of some things last forever.

That's the feeling I got when my friend Chaya S. called me the other day. Chaya is a friend of mine who made aliyah a few years ago from Brooklyn, New York, with her family. They live near the Mattersdorf neighborhood in Jerusalem, and so she travels a lot on the #3 bus.

The route of the #3 bus includes many "ultra-Orthodox" neighborhoods, and so the bus is usually filled with frum-looking men and women. But the bus drivers on that route are usually not noticeably religious.

ALL YEAR LONG

This past *Chol HaMoed Sukkot*, Chaya started crying on the bus: she just couldn't believe her eyes. But then again, the fact that she *did* see and believe what she saw on the bus is probably what made her cry in the first place. Only in Israel.

The driver on the #3 bus that day was not outwardly religious-looking. Chaya was sitting just a few seats away from him.

The bus wasn't too crowded, though many of the men were carefully carrying their *lulavim* and *etrogim*.

At the bus stop of Kiryat Sanz, one of the passengers who got on was gingerly carrying his *lulav* and *etrog*. Whatever the conversation was that he had with the bus driver, the latter suddenly shut off the motor, and got off the bus with this man.

Intrigued, Chaya looked out of the bus window, as did many of the other passengers.

What did they see?

Standing at the bus stop, the non-religious-looking bus driver was saying the blessings over the passenger's *lulav* and *etrog*. I guess the man had asked the bus driver if he had done so yet.

What can you say?

It's the Simple Deeds

You know those little children's books that we read our children — the ones that tell of "simple" men in ages past whose simple deeds, though unbeknownst to them, turned out to be responsible for saving the entire *shtetl*?

I think of those little storybooks sometimes when I'm riding on the bus in Jerusalem.

And I wonder....

Of course, some things have become so usual, that one barely notices them anymore. Like the Chasidim who invariably help women they don't even know, carry their baby carriages up and/or down the back steps of the bus. Men who, of course, wouldn't look at or talk to these women strangers, or sit next to them on the bus. But, they will seize a chance to help them.

And there are other things, too.

Like the kids who try to look "American" by sporting earrings, undershirts rolled all the way up at the sleeves, and funny-looking butch hair-cuts.

But, boy oh boy — when an elderly man or woman gets on the bus! So often you will see them jump up to give away their seat. Without a thought. Just a Jewish instinct at work.

Baruch HaShem.

That's what I thought about the other day as I watched a scantily clad Israeli girl on the bus jump up to give her seat to a man with a long white beard.

By her dress, she disagreed with his life style. By her dress, she probably cared little for it, and understood it even less.

But in a bus that wasn't even very crowded, she got up for him immediately.

And who knows....

May HaShem look at these many "little" acts of respect and kindness, and judge us favorably.

"Street Behavior"

My seventeen-year-old daughter came home from school the other day, and, as we were talking, she casually mentioned a certain not-terribly-unusual "daily occurrence" which happened on her bus-ride home.

Usually, the bus is fairly full, with people returning from a busy day, hungry, tired, and wanting to get home.

This time, after everyone was aboard and the bus was ready to leave the bus-stop, a very, very, very old woman wanted to get on.

As she started slowly climbing up the steps of the bus, the old woman kept calling out, "Rega, rega!" ("One minute! One minute!") to the bus driver, since she was nervous that the bus was going to start moving before she got settled.

As the (very) old woman was moving very slowly, and kept constantly repeating, in a panicky voice, "One minute! One minute!" the bus driver kept reassuring her, "Don't worry. Don't worry, Savta [Grandma]. Take your time. I'm waiting."

Still calling out, "Rega, rega!", the very old woman finally got up the steps, with the bus driver constantly reassuring her each time, "Don't worry, don't worry. I'm waiting."

Someone of course vacated the first seat in the bus for her, and, after quite a while, the old woman was finally seated.

It was only at this point that the bus driver turned around in his seat, and asked her, "Is everything all right? Are you ready?"

The old woman answered, "Yes."

And so, the bus driver turned back to

his steering wheel, and, off they all went.

I guess I don't need to add that, obviously, no one on the crowded bus griped, complained, or said anything about the delay.

And, what struck me so much about this was that, *Baruch HaShem*, this is the kind of "street behavior" that my daughter is being exposed to all the time — without my even being aware of it.

Where's Mine?

Though living in Israel for only three or four years, my friend Peshy S. is really getting into the swing of things. And Peshy, you must know, was the type of person who never talked to anyone on the streets whom she didn't know — before getting acclimated to life in Israel, that is.

Five days a week Peshy takes the #2 bus to work. After a while, you get to recognize the bus drivers' faces, and they yours.

But of course Peshy never said anything to them, except "Thank you" as they gave her back her bus ticket after punching it.

Which makes this story so special....

One morning Peshy got up late. So, instead of eating breakfast, she just grabbed a lollipop and ran out the door to catch her bus.

As the bus driver handed her back her bus ticket, Peshy took the lollipop out of her mouth to thank him.

The bus driver looked at Peshy, and then asked, "Where's mine?" (lollipop, that is).

I thought that was cute....

And the next day, when Peshy boarded the #2 bus, she handed the bus driver his very own lollipop.

I thought that was very cute....

And then, Peshy told me, the bus driver unwrapped his lollipop, said thank you, and put it into his mouth.

Can you imagine the reaction of the early-morning, going-to-work people boarding the bus at the next bus stop upon seeing the bus driver sucking a lollipop?

What a fun place to live!

Do You Have Change?

With Israel's rising inflation, the denominations of our paper money are getting bigger, too.

When I first made aliyah, many, many years ago, the highest denomination of the (then) lira was 50, if I remember correctly. Today, besides the currency going Jewish (i.e., returning to the shekel), we have a 100 as well as a 200 shekel bill (which feels like a *lot* of money at one shot)! In fact, sometimes shopkeepers don't even have the change to cash a 200 shekel bill, as happened the other day at our local falafel store.

While waiting in line to place my order, I saw the cashier suddenly start waving a 200 shekel note in the air high above his head. "Does anyone have change for a 200?" he called out to the crowd. When it was ascertained that no one did, he reached across his cash-register, handed the 200 shekel bill to a little boy who was waiting to pay, and asked him to please run next door to the vegetable store and see if they had change. (Which of course the boy did — his place in line being saved for him while other customers paid and left.)

This (fairly common) occurrence flashed through my mind this week while I was sitting on the #2 bus, returning home from work.

The bus was caught in traffic near a traffic light. Suddenly a Chasidic man jumped out of his parked car, and ran in front of the waiting bus, around to the driver's side.

Sticking his hand up to the driver's open window, he waved a 200 shekel bill at the driver, asking if the driver could change it.

While the traffic light stayed red (this Land is *full* of miracles), the driver counted out the change.

That each should trust the other in case the light did change, was also fascinating to me. But that someone in a car should even *think* of asking a bus driver, via the driver's window, to give him change, was really something.

(Though it is surprising why I should have been so shocked: Israeli bus drivers are always stopping each other, especially when they are traveling in opposite directions down two-way streets. Besides simply sending regards, often they are also sticking their heads and arms out of their windows, waving money, asking each other if they have change. Why not?)

What a country!

It's Only Fair

Jerusalem offers a unique bus ride which lasts over an hour and a half. It is a city bus tour, the #99, that encircles the city of Jerusalem.

As the bus passes the many historical/religious/modern sites that people from all over the world are so interested in seeing, the #99-bus driver keeps up a running commentary, briefly describing what is being seen.

The bus is also air-conditioned, has those specially padded, not too uncomfortable seats, and the entire excursion costs less than $5.00.

And, to repeat, it lasts almost two

hours....

Well, since I must admit that I have not really "done" anything with my young daughter this summer, and since I am getting older and thus more and more appreciative of the sedentary pastimes, and since this bus tour *was* one of the items on my "things-to-do-together-this-summer" list, and, since it was Tishah b'Av and this could be a good way to focus on the destruction of the Temple, well, since it was *very* hot outside, and our air-conditioner at home was broken, this really seemed the perfect time to try this air-conditioned tour of our Holy City of Jerusalem.

Luckily for us, one of the bus-stops for this #99 bus was right across the street from where we were standing after shul.

All we had to do was wait for it to come, since, though the tour really, officially, starts at Mamilla (near Jaffa Gate), you can join the bus tour (and leave it) at any of the stops along its circuitous route.

This is the kind of family outing I can handle. So we waited. In the hot sun.

Finally, *Baruch HaShem*, when I had just declared that I wasn't going to wait anymore, and that this was getting ridiculous, the #99 bus came.

Ooh, the blessed relief of that air-conditioning!

It was very pleasant sitting there, watching Avshalom's *kever* going by, and hearing about the Mount of Olives and the Israeli soldiers recapturing the Old City of Jerusalem through Lion's Gate on our right ... and it was so delightfully cool.

Well, about six minutes after we joined the bus-tour, the driver pulls into his starting/ending point, announces that the tour will continue in fourteen minutes, shuts off the bus's motor, and prepares to get off the bus.

(You realize, of course, that means he shut off the air-conditioning, too.)

In response to our queries, the bus

IT'S ONLY FAIR

driver explained that the tour would continue after his break — he's been driving and tour-explaining-talking for almost two hours straight. We can leave the bus if we want to; we should just hold onto our tickets and come back on time.

He didn't understand. It was hot out there. And there was nowhere to sit, and no shade, and I was getting thirsty, and I didn't want to move.

We asked if he could please leave the air-conditioning on, since it was a very hot day. He explained that he couldn't, since he couldn't leave the bus with its motor on, unattended. I must admit that it made sense, but I figured I'd try anyway....

After a few more minutes' discussion back and forth with him, I announced, "It's hot, it's Tishah b'Av, and I've only been on this tour five minutes. I think I deserve my money back. It's not fair to make us wait in this heat."

He and I both knew that my getting my money back was out of the question

— and even if I did, there was nowhere to go since there were no other buses nearby. He therefore just repeated that there was nothing he could do, and he left.

Half a minute later, an old man climbed onto the bus, started the motor (and the air-conditioning), spread out his newspaper by leaning it against the bus's large steering wheel, and began reading his newspaper. Without a word or a comment.

After seven or eight minutes he looked around at us, said not to touch anything, took his newspaper, and left the bus. With the motor and the air-conditioning running. I guess he figured he could trust us.

When the driver finally returned to his cool bus, he didn't say a word (yes, we then thanked him after he got settled).

Jews have good hearts. It was a perfect occurrence for Tishah b'Av.... May HaShem see our *ahavat chinnam* [boundless love], count it as our making amends for our past *sinat chinnam* [causeless hatred], and rebuild the Temple speedily in our days.

Time for Minchah

The following story took place in Jerusalem, during *Chol HaMoed Sukkot*.

Rivki S. was going to the Kotel to *daven Minchah*. Since there are always a lot of people going to the Kotel during Chol HaMoed, Egged (Jerusalem's bus company) usually puts a lot of extra buses on the #2 bus-line.

Everything was fine on Rivki's bus until it reached the outskirts of the Old City walls near Har HaZeitim [the Mount of Olives]. Suddenly the traffic stopped, and didn't move.

And didn't move. And didn't move.

TIME FOR MINCHAH

Of course, the bus was packed with people, and after a while many started getting restless.

But there was nowhere to go and nothing to do; just to sit in the bus and wait.

It's still not clear if this massive traffic jam was caused by a traffic accident on the narrow streets, or if it was simply a result of the thousands and thousands of people in cars and buses flocking to the Kotel to *daven*.

But one thing was clear. It was getting late, and the bus was not moving.

It was at this point that some of the men on the bus began getting even more than a little nervous.

There was nowhere to get out of the bus (the street was too narrow and too full of traffic), and nowhere to go, even if they could have gotten out of the bus.

And time was passing quickly — very quickly — and soon it would be the latest time possible for being able to *daven Minchah*.

That's when one of the men called out — in the crowded, city bus — "*Minchah! Minchah!* In the back of the bus."

The passengers then began a transfer of populations — all the women moved towards the front of the bus, and all the men moved to the rear.

It was quite orderly, with no one objecting or staying on the "wrong side" of the bus.

And so the men *davened Minchah*. And many of the women joined in, from the "women's section."

And the bus driver didn't start that bus moving until everyone had finished *daven*ing. On a regular, public, city bus.

Nice, huh?!

By Cab...

The Palace Entrance

Although the neighborhood of Ramot is only a twelve-minute drive from my Jerusalem apartment, it is reached by a highway on which I rarely travel.

In fact, I hadn't traveled to Ramot in several years. But there is one thing that everyone who lives in or visits Jerusalem knows: "Blessed are You... *boneh* [builder of] Yerushalayim" is *not* an empty phrase!

The last time I had seen Ramot, there were bare mountains everywhere. There was only one apartment complex in the entire area — an "egg-box" looking affair which had won a World Expo design award in Canada several years earlier.

I was thus happy that I had to go to Ramot for a meeting — the area had probably been built up quite a bit during the years I had not seen it.

When the cab picked me up, it made me sad to see the young Israeli cab driver. He was wearing a white undershirt with the sleeves rolled up to his shoulders, had funny-looking "punk" hair, and wore an earring in one ear.

What a pity, I told myself. Though I know we are not supposed to judge a person by his outward appearance, it was very sad to see a Jew so very far from his heritage.

As the cab driver zoomed along the highway, Ramot suddenly loomed up in the distance. The mountain directly in front of me, as well as the mountains on both my right and left sides, were all *filled* — actually stuffed — with gorgeous apartment buildings. The most impres-

THE PALACE ENTRANCE

sive architecture I'd seen in years. Thousands upon thousands of beautiful apartments filled with thousands upon thousands of Jewish families, as far as the eye could see.

The beauty of it — the magnitude of it — actually took my breath away, and I gasped.

"*Baruch HaShem*," I blurted out. "It is so beautiful!"

At which point the earring-clad young driver turned to me and said, "What do you expect, *Geveret*! You are in Jerusalem. This is the *prozdor* [entrance-hall] of the Palace. The *prozdor* of the King."

Silly me. Of course it would be beautiful.

Wishing You More

One learns so much about proper attitudes towards life from people in the streets of Israel. Daily life here really brings new meaning to the phrase "Open University"...

My friend Sara W. was on her way to a wedding. Since she hadn't found a babysitter, she brought three of her children with her. (That's another one of the amazing things about life in Israel: in a country where people's salary checks appear considerably lower than those in America or England, most wedding reception/dinner invitations are sent without reply cards. And, by common consent, an invitation to you includes your children, parents, grandparents, and/or anyone else you feel like bringing along to share in the *simchah*.)

Sara and her children all piled into the taxi-cab, and had soon traveled the short distance to the wedding hall.

As Sara went to pay the taxi-cab driver, she found that the only money she had with her in her pocketbook was a bill of a very large denomination... ridiculously large, especially considering the short trip they had just made.

Realizing that this meant that the cab driver would have to give her back an inordinately large amount of change — perhaps even all the change he had on him — Sara apologized for giving him such a big bill.

The taxi-cab driver's response?

"May the Almighty give you a *brachah* that you should always have only large denominations of money!"

What an Apology

I know that everyone, everywhere, is nice to a *kallah* [a bride]. But somehow, in Israel, I think it's a little more. (In fact, *everything* in Israel, I think, is a little more!)

My friend Shandee M. was telling me about a trip to the Kotel she made with a friend of hers the other day.

Her friend, Jill, was going to be married that evening. Since Jill had come on *aliyah* by herself, and had no family in Israel, her friend Shandee was spending the day accompanying Jill wherever she needed to go.

Jill decided that she wanted to *daven*

WHAT AN APOLOGY

her wedding-day *Minchah* at the Kotel. So, calling a taxi-cab, off they went.

On the way to the Kotel they discussed a "package-price" with the cab driver. The agreed-upon price included a ride to the Kotel and back home, with a fifteen-minute wait for *daven*ing *Minchah*.

Well, it took Jill longer than fifteen minutes to finish *daven*ing.

By the time they returned to the taxi-cab, the driver was fuming.

As Jill and Shandee piled into the cab, the driver yelled at them, complaining about the time he had been forced to wait, commenting that he could have gotten another fare in the meantime, and that he was losing money on this deal.

While apologizing, Shandee explained that Jill was getting married that night, and that, as a *kallah*, her *Minchah* prayer was longer than usual.

Well, that was enough for the Israeli cab driver!

He immediately changed his entire

attitude and began to apologize profusely. In addition to his repeated wishes of *"Mazal tov,"* he kept apologizing for yelling at a bride on her wedding day.

As they neared Jill's apartment, the cab driver came up with something else.

"Let me make it up to you," he said. "As a wedding present, I will drive you from your home to the wedding hall. My gift to you."

Jill had already made other arrangements, but, boy, what a country!

Normal Crazy Day

There really cannot be any other place on earth with so many opportunities for real *simchah* [joy]. I mean, almost anything you do in Israel leaves you open to that deep, satisfied happiness you get from a meaningful encounter.

You see, it happened again to me today. I got into a cab for a simple ride, and ended up ... well, let me start at the beginning.

Once a week, for 2 – 3 hours, I have an *ozeret* [cleaning lady] come to my home. Since her grandson was having his *chalakah* [the traditional celebration of a boy's first haircut at age three], she invited me to come. It was to be on Lag ba'Omer, at the gravesite of Shmuel HaNavi, the Prophet Samuel. A fifteen-minute cab drive away from my home. And no bus service as far as I could tell.

Having moved to Israel over twenty-five years ago, I accepted it as completely normal that my cleaning lady would invite me to attend her family get-together.

And, knowing her, I knew that she would get real happiness in seeing that I would take the time to come. No idle invitation, this.

So I called a cab, and went.

Everything normal up to here, yes?

I arranged with the secular, non-yarmulke wearing cab driver to take me there, wait 10 – 15 minutes, and then return me to my starting point.

We agreed upon a price, and off we went — to the gravesite of Samuel the Prophet.

NORMAL CRAZY DAY

On the way there we discussed a little politics. And upon arrival, I invited him to come in and have a soda while he waited (living in Israel so long, I'm becoming like the native Sabras — I *know* my *ozeret* would have been angry at me if I hadn't invited him in).

He took a few seconds to get out of the cab, and then I noticed that he had put a blue velvet yarmulke on his head. Though a "non-religious" Israeli, I guess he felt that he was going to a holy place....

My *ozeret*'s sister suggested I go down to the actual grave of the Prophet Samuel for a few minutes while they waited for the hair-cutting ceremony to begin.

So I did. Down lots of narrow, steep, stone steps.

After a quick, heartfelt prayer, I began my trek back upstairs, only to see my still-yarmulke-wearing cab driver coming *down* the steps, towards the grave.

"One minute," he said. "As long as

we're here... okay?"

Of course I told him to take as long as he wanted, it was fine with me.

And then, after heart-felt Mazal tovs to my ozeret and her family, I returned to the cab — from whence the cab driver gave me a bottle of water from the trunk of his car... kept there for cases when passengers visited a grave and wanted to do the customary hand-washing afterwards.

On the way home we discussed how daily political life in Israel keeps pointing to the fact that we can't rely on anything except the Almighty. And by the time we got to my home, he wanted to get a few tapes from Arachim of Rabbi Amnon Yitzhak dealing with the uniqueness of the Jewish people and the fact that we always seem to fight among ourselves.

Somehow, as I walked towards my door, I realized that only in Israel could I have such a normal, crazy day.

You Never Know

Living in Jerusalem, I've never felt the need to own a car. The bus system is very good, and, when necessary, or if I feel lazy, I take a cab.

This also leaves me open to many interesting experiences.

Like several months ago, when I had one of those double-whammy evenings — a Bar Mitzvah and a wedding on the same night. Since they were being held at opposite ends of town, I figured I just wouldn't go to the wedding, which was further away. But, as I left the Bar Mitzvah, I walked directly in front of a taxi stand.

Well, I mean, how easy can HaShem make it to do a mitzvah?

Feeling a little like a *tzaddekes*, I decided to splurge: the wedding was *way* out in the middle of nowhere, and I knew I would never find a cab out there — you had to walk 15 – 20 minutes just to find a bus! So, I decided to take a cab there, have him wait fifteen minutes while I said *Mazal tov*, and then bring me to my home.

The man in the taxi booth gave me a reasonable price and, since the one I thought was the taxi driver seemed to be nice, I had no qualms driving alone in the taxi-cab with him — even though I had never used this taxi company before, and it was a long trip, on a very dark night, and the way to the wedding was along winding, unlit, dark, and empty roads.

After thanking the dispatcher, I started walking towards the parked taxi-cab. And who walks out of the office and gets behind the wheel of my taxi-cab? A young man with hair that is slicked-back and heavily greased, sporting long fingernails, an earring, and wearing his undershirt rolled up at the sleeves until his shoulders.

I just couldn't think of a nice way out of it at this point, so I just reminded HaShem that I was on my way to do a mitzvah, got into the cab, and off we went.

We started speeding along, and soon left the lights of civilization far behind. As I marveled at the distance we had traveled, and the beauty of the stillness on the mountain roads with the flickering lights in the darkness far behind us, I forgot myself (and who I was with) and exclaimed, "Is this really still Jerusalem?" (i.e., has Jerusalem grown so much?!).

My long-nailed, greased-back-hair cab driver answered simply, "Yes, it is. They only keep one day of *Purim* — *Shushan Purim* — out here, like most of

Jerusalem. However, in Ramot [another far-flung section of Jerusalem], there are sections where there's a *she'elah* about a second-day Megillah reading...."

Taken aback wasn't the word for it. Quite a people.

Part II:
Being There

DAILY LIFE...

"Gut Yom Tov"

There are so many things in Israel that are special: so many little extras that you don't expect or even conceive of, until you hear about them.

Like the 24-hour-a-day emergency beeper systems. The ones for the elderly or for people with pacemakers.

I mean, anyone would imagine that an emergency 24-hour beeper system would basically be the same anywhere in the world. At least, that's what my friend Chana K. thought.

Her eighty-five-year-old mother had come to live in Israel ten years previously. Though Chana's father *(z"l)* had died several years later, Chana's mother didn't want to leave their apartment, and so she lived alone.

After her mother fell while making breakfast alone one morning in her Bayit Vegan apartment in Jerusalem, Chana was able to convince her to sign up for a 24-hour emergency beeper system; the kind you wear pinned to your clothing like a piece of jewelry.

With this system, the head office calls the beeper wearer two or three times throughout the year just to check that the system is working properly.

So, when Chana's mother received a call from them a few days before Shavuot, she wasn't very surprised... until she realized that the only reason the head office of the emergency 24-hour beeper service was calling her was to give her holiday greetings, and to wish her — in Yiddish — *"Gut Yom Tov."*

Again and Again

My friend Yehudit P. was telling me about her pre-6:00 A.M. walks early Friday mornings. The quiet is thunderous, the whole atmosphere ethereal. And then, just as the owner is opening up his hole-in-the-wall pita-bread bakery store in the Bukharan market of Jerusalem, Yehudit arrives to buy freshly baked Syrian-style pita (made by throwing the dough against the inside of his hole-in-the-wall oven).

Over the months, Yehudit has come to be impressed by this chubby, bald, Syrian Jew's kindness. Which makes what he said to Yehudit one morning so

AGAIN AND AGAIN

understandable....

Yehudit had arrived a little late, and so she took her place in line, behind another woman buying pita.

This woman was an old, Bukharan woman, bent with age, wearing a floral-patterned babushka. She seemed to be very dissatisfied with the pita-bread that the Syrian-Jew was offering her.

"No, this one is burnt," she said, handing it back to the baker. "It's not good. I want a different one."

So the man gave her a different one.

After carefully examining it, the woman returned this one too, commenting, "This one doesn't look well-done enough. Give me another...."

As Yehudit stood in the growing line, awaiting her turn, she marveled at the patience of this simple baker. For it seemed that, each time the man handed the old woman a perfectly good, fresh, warm pita-bread, the old woman would carefully examine it, and then hand it back, with some complaint.

As the old woman returned yet another pita to the baker, he finally said to her a bit firmly, "It's okay, *Geveret*. This one is good. It's a very good one. It's fine, they're all fine."

Convinced, and wrapping her six large pita-breads in a small blanket to keep them warm, the little old lady finally walked away.

Turning to Yehudit, the baker apologized for the delay, and explained, "I feel bad that I got so agitated with her. You see, she doesn't pay."

Help on the Street

Israel has been in turmoil lately with the *bushah* [shame] of some Jews talking about giving away to goyim pieces of Land which the Almighty gave us. As a public show of "crying in the streets to Heaven," a huge demonstration was held in Jerusalem some time ago. My friend's daughter was at that demonstration.

The crowd was so huge (estimated at over 200,000 Jews), that there were places where the air was stuffy, even though everyone was outside in the open air.

After saying *Tehillim* over the microphone system, *Kaddish* was said, with thousands upon thousands answering appropriately. Then speeches began.

At some point, the crowd started moving, and my friend's daughter, who is fairly short, was crushed in the crowd. With the huge numbers of people, and the stuffiness of the air, she soon fainted.

When she woke up, she was in an ambulance. A stranger had picked her up and somehow carried her through the crowd, over to where the ambulances awaited any emergencies.

They were going to take her to the hospital, but my friend's daughter did not want to go. She just wanted to go home.

When another stranger saw that she didn't have any money with her, but only a ticket to take the bus, 25 shekels was forced on her so that she could get home in a taxi-cab.

"How can I pay you back?" she asked the person whom she had never seen before in her life. "Please give me your name and address so that I can send the money back to you."

The stranger's answer: "Give it to *tzedakah*."

It's Nice To Hear

We all know that we are supposed to judge our fellow Jews favorably [*dan lechaf zechut*]. Many of us go to *shiurim* to teach us why, most of us read about it to understand how and when, and all of us know how important it is.

Of course, we all expect our Rabbis, teachers, and *gedolim* to display adherence to this Torah injunction. We also assume it is practiced by our children's educators and our friends; and, we try, too. But it is particularly nice when we see "regular" people judging us favorably, even under adverse circumstances.

Such a *dan lechaf zechut* situation

happened to my friend Adelle B. the other day.

It was *erev Yom Tov*, and her neighbor couldn't get a taxi-cab. Since she really needed to get to Meah Shearim, Adelle offered to drive her.

In the *erev Yom Tov* rush, and, knowing she was only going to drop the woman off seconds from where they lived, and then return straight home, Adelle just grabbed her car keys and ran out of her apartment, without bothering to take her purse.

Within three minutes the neighbor was dropped off, and Adelle started the return journey home, through the narrow streets of Meah Shearim.

At one point, as she was stopped by traffic in the narrow street, a beggar leaned over Adelle's lowered car window, and asked for some *tzedakah*.

Adelle, behind the wheel of her station wagon without her purse, apologized that she didn't have any money with her.

The beggar hurried to reassure her: "Don't worry, *Geveret*. It's okay. I'll be all right. Just have a good Yom Tov, and don't feel bad."

What can one say?

Mind Your Own Business

I work with a lovely young woman named Yocheved L. She and her husband came to Israel from Boro Park one or two years ago.

One of the things about Israel that amazes Yocheved is the way Israelis get involved with everyone and everything around them. A case in point is this story that happened to a friend of hers who was visiting from Brooklyn.

This friend had a cousin in Jerusalem who desperately needed a babysitter for a few hours one afternoon. And so Yocheved's friend offered to go and babysit for her baby cousin whom she had not yet seen.

The baby was sleeping when the

mother had to leave, and all looked quiet. But when the baby awoke crying, and didn't see her mother, and instead saw a stranger she'd never seen before, well, as you can imagine, that baby started screaming and screaming and screaming.

Yocheved's friend did everything she could think of to get the baby to stop screaming: she rocked her, she sang to her, she jiggled her, she changed her diaper, she tried to give her a bottle, etc. — all to no avail. The baby just kept screaming and screaming and screaming.

Suddenly there was a knock at the front door.

Carrying the screaming infant, Yocheved's friend went to answer it. True, in Brooklyn she'd never open the door to a complete stranger, but this was Jerusalem, and the apartment was on the third floor, without an elevator,... and with the baby screaming and screaming and screaming....

A woman was standing there. She

MIND YOUR OWN BUSINESS

walked into the apartment, and explained matter-of-factly that she'd heard a baby crying and had come to help. She took the screaming baby into her arms, and proceeded to quiet it down. When the baby finally stopped crying, the lady handed the baby back, and left.

When the mother returned soon afterwards, Yocheved's friend told her about the nice neighbor who had heard the crying and had come to help. The mother was appreciative... and it wasn't until several days later that Yocheved heard the whole story.

It wasn't a neighbor who had come in to help.

A stranger had been passing on the street — three flights below — and had heard the crying of a Jewish baby.

This stranger climbed three flights of stairs to go into someone else's apartment to offer to help.

And she did.

Because there are no "strangers" among Jews in our own Land.

Mazal Tov!

One of the joys of life in Israel is the daily interaction one experiences on the streets ... and how people care for (i.e., get involved with) each other. It brings to life the expression *kol Yisrael arevim zeh lazeh* [all Israel is responsible one for another].

My daughter Pnina K. experienced this exchange a few years ago:

The girls from a Bais Yaacov high school had just been let out for the day. Suddenly, not too far from the school, two seventeen-year-old girls grabbed each other on the street and started shrieking and jumping up and down.

A woman passed by, and gave them a look as if to say, "That's not a nice way to behave on the street." But they were too busy screaming to notice.

Pnina had been walking towards the woman. Since she knew the story behind the screams, as she reached the concerned woman, Pnina explained, "Their good friend just got engaged."

Instead of being taken aback, or being insulted or apologetic, the woman immediately exclaimed, "Oh, *Mazal tov*! *Mazal tov*!" with real joy in her voice.

It was a good lesson in judging *lechaf zechut*, and an even better lesson on how people are concerned about the behavior of fellow Jews, as if they were members of their own family.

And it gave Pnina a nice feeling to see how happy the woman became upon learning about a *simchah* in *klal Yisrael*.

You Can Cross Now

When I told my friend Channie P. that I was looking for stories that showed glimpses of life in Israel, she immediately had a few to tell me.

Then, after a moment of thought, she added, "I saw something today that might be appropriate for you. But I'm not so sure — maybe not — it's not so particularly spectacular."

And she proceeded to tell me about what she had seen....

It was at the busy intersection of Yakim and Shmuel HaNavi Streets. Cars whoosh by quite quickly, and it can be a dangerous crosswalk.

An old man stood on the sidewalk, obviously wanting to get to the other side of the street, but he was afraid to cross.

As Channie watched, a driver stopped his car, and motioned for the old man to cross.

The old man must not have noticed the driver, for he continued standing on the very edge of the sidewalk.

The driver kept waving and waving from his car, trying to catch the old man's attention and let him know that he could safely cross the street now. But the old man just didn't notice.

Finally, the driver got out of his car, went up to the old man, gently took his arm, and walked with him all the way to the other side of the street. He then returned to his car, and drove off.

I couldn't get over this moving story.

But Channie was surprised by my reaction.

"It's not so unusual," she said. "People used to do that all the time for my Avigail when she was little."

Time To Daven

Yossi S., my friend's husband, told me about this next incident. It was told to him by one of the participants, a boy studying in the Lakewood Yeshivah in Itri, on Sorotzkin Street in Jerusalem. (Yossi and his family moved here from Flatbush, New York, eight-and-a-half years ago.)

It was during the time of the demonstrations against building a new, major road in the French Hill section of Jerusalem. The men of the Yeshivah world were gathering en masse each day to protest the road's construction in that site, which would require the removal of Jewish bones from ancient graves and their reburial elsewhere.

Five Lakewood yeshivah boys piled into their friend's car one afternoon to drive to the protest-demonstration in French Hill, in order to lend their support in more than just thought.

Before getting to the area where the demonstration was taking place, they had to drive along the main thoroughfare of Bar Ilan Street, which runs through a secular neighborhood.

Suddenly the yeshivah boys noticed a group of policemen standing by the side of the road, lights from their police-cars flashing.

As cars zoomed by, a policeman picked out the yeshivah boys, and waved them over to stop and park their car.

The yeshiva boys were wondering if this meant that they were getting arrested already, in order to prevent them from taking part in the nearby protest-demonstration, since, because of their dress, it was obvious that they were extremely religious.

As the boys piled out of their car, a policeman approached them.

"Have you *daven*ed Minchah yet?" he asked.

These policemen needed a *minyan* right then because they were afraid that, once the protest-demonstration got under way, they might get too involved, and not have time to *daven*.

All in a Day's Work

Life in Israel is life filled with action. You just have to keep your eyes open.

I have a friend named Chayah B. who made aliyah awhile ago. She's getting used to the idea that if you watch and listen to what is going on around you, there is never a dull moment here.

Chayah works in the Old City of Jerusalem. Five days a week she travels to work by bus. It lets her off outside the Kotel area, near a large parking lot, minutes from her office....

Living in Israel, one gets used to seeing soldiers. They are everywhere. Guns slung over their shoulders, khaki shirts unbuttoned a few buttons at the collar and half-tucked into their baggy pants. Young boys. Older men. On duty at public buildings, supermarkets, and at the Kotel... on guard — *hishtadlus* — to help protect us.

Every day Chayah passes the guards checking packages, purses, and people going into the Old City via the entrance near the Kotel. So she's gotten used to them, and they to her. And, of course, each wishes the other a "Good morning," and a "Good afternoon," as Chayah goes in and out each day.

Sometimes the soldiers are busy checking lines of people, sometimes they are talking among themselves, and sometimes they are learning Gemara as they sit and wait. But always they are soldiers, ready to act....

Which made it even more striking to Chayah one day when, getting off the bus, she saw three soldiers congregated around a passenger car, far from the throngs of people milling around. Two soldiers were standing by the back of the car, and another was standing next to the driver's open window. All the soldiers were talking, and the two at the back were wildly gesticulating with their arms.

After watching for a moment, Chayah realized what the trouble was: the woman driver had been unable to maneuver her car into the parking place, and the soldiers, walking by, had stopped to help her park her car.

Doing It Right

I was walking down the street several years ago, on my way to buy a few new plants. There is a lovely plant nursery two-and-a-half blocks from my apartment, on the other side of a busy intersection. I have to cross two streets to get there.

Though I wasn't in a particular hurry, when I missed the green light at my corner, I didn't wait to cross at the crosswalk, but continued walking along the sidewalk.

Approximately half-way down the street, I checked that there were no cars coming from either direction (I'm a responsible person), and then I crossed in the middle of the block.

I continued walking along, towards the next intersection.

An old woman was slowly walking towards me, coming from the opposite direction. As we came abreast of each other, she stopped me.

"Excuse me, *Geveret*," she said. "You think you crossed the street safely, because nothing happened to you, *Baruch HaShem*. But know that, *because* nothing happened to you, it is possible that you have reduced some of your reward in *Shamayim* [Heaven]. HaShem uses up some of the reward a person was to have received for doing *mitzvot* when He has to do miracles to protect that person in this world, in *olam hazeh*."

And with that, the old woman continued on her way.

And now I always cross at crosswalks, and try to wait for green lights.

And I marvel at how wonderful it is to have regular people on the streets thinking so clearly — and willing to share those thoughts with others.

Hope You Don't Mind

My friend Shira's oldest daughter, Rita, got married two years ago. Last year Rita gave birth during *Chol HaMoed Sukkot*.

It was a hard labor and delivery, which lasted two days. Her husband Nachum stayed with her at the hospital almost all of the time.

Being Sukkot, of course he wanted to eat all his meals and snacks in a *sukkah*.

And, of course, being Israel, hospitals have *sukkah*s on their premises (as do restaurants, most major municipal parks, and sundry other places).

Perhaps a story like this one can happen anywhere — but I kind of doubt it....

Nachum had just washed for *haMotzi,* the blessing over bread. As he was walking towards the door which would lead to the hospital's *sukkah*, a man came up to him and, in a quiet voice, whispered, "I'm not sure, but it is *possible* that there might be a *she'elah* [halachic question] regarding the *sechach* of the hospital's *sukkah*."

This man didn't realize that Rita's husband couldn't ask for details — he wasn't allowed to speak — since he had already washed his hands but had not yet made the blessing over the bread.

So... what could Nachum do?

He left the hospital, without speaking. He walked out of the door, and across the street.

Stopping at the first *sukkah* he came to, Rita's husband opened the door, walked in, sat down, and made the blessings. (People in Israel often erect their sukkahs on the sidewalk, directly in front of their apartment buildings, when they don't have private *sukkah* porches.)

Just as Nachum was taking a second bite of his bread, the *sukkah*'s door opened again. And this time, in walked the owner, carrying his own food.

"*Chag Sameach*. Welcome!" was all the man said, as he arranged his own food around that of his uninvited "guest," and smiled at this stranger sitting in his *sukkah*.

Shopping...

Morning Shopping Spree

I hope I never get used to the fact that Israel is a really weird country to live in. Since I came here right after college, over twenty-five years ago, I consider myself an expert.

Take the Israeli concept of shopping. In the U.S., if a store is closed, it is closed. You go away and come back later, or else you just go somewhere else to shop.

Not here in Israel.

A few mornings ago, I ran out of bread while making my daughter's sandwiches for school. It was 6:45 A.M., and, not wanting to bother my neighbors, and knowing that the *makolet* [small neighborhood grocery store] was open very early in the morning, I ran out to buy a sliced bread.

The men were returning home from morning prayers, and a neighbor, Professor M., passed by. From where I stood, I could see that the store was completely dark — with no one inside.

In disappointment, I turned away. Professor M. asked what was wrong. When I said I needed bread, the dignified professor said casually, "Go around back and take a loaf. The delivery truck has probably been here already."

I was shocked (but went to the back of the store anyway). Cases of milk were standing around, as were cardboard delivery cartons full of bread and rolls — all stacked in front of the iron grate of the grocery store's locked back door.

And, leaning over the carton of fresh rolls, was our neighbor, Dr. S. And, slowly walking away, with a bag of milk in his hands, was elderly Mr. B., a respected member of the community.

In the far distance, I saw the store

owner slowly making his way to the store. I waited for him, because I couldn't believe this whole scene.

As he started opening up the back door to begin bringing his crates inside, he smiled in greeting as another member of our community walked off with several rolls.

I paid for my sliced bread, and asked the store owner if this goes on every morning.

He explained that he opens his store after the men return from morning prayers. Therefore they take what they need out back from that morning's delivery, and their wives come in later in the day to pay.

I marveled at our community, and at this crazy country where such things can go on. And at an Israeli small grocery store owner, who runs a business that way — trusting that everyone, a Jew after all, will make good his "purchase" later on.

What a country!

Upon the Doorpost

Harriet G. and her husband made aliyah about four years ago with their eight children. That's long enough ago for Harriet to have become acclimated to many of the facets of daily life in Israel.

But I guess kids keep their sharp-eyed outlook longer....

Harriet had taken the children to the new, huge shopping mall in Jerusalem's Malcha neighborhood.

The entire family was impressed by the beauty of the interior design, the vast number of stores, and the multi-leveled extravaganza of glass elevators, never-ending escalators, and a huge glass-domed rotunda.

The fact that everyone there spoke

Hebrew wasn't anything special (though Harriet still gets a little twinge of pride when hearing her two smallest ones rattle on in the holy tongue).

The fact that all the restaurants and fast-food eateries were kosher, many of them *mehadrin*, was as it should be.

But the fact that all the dairy restaurants were located down one wing of the concourse, and all the meat eateries were located down a completely different side of the concourse, was quite impressive.

However, what made it really something to write about was the fact that a large sign was posted at the intersection of the two eating-wings.

One arrow pointed down the left concourse, and announced: *besari* [meat]. Here were found hamburger stands, Moroccan, Hungarian, and other types of *fleishig* food restaurants, shwarma stands, and much more.

Another arrow pointed to the right concourse, and announced: *chalavi* [dairy].

Along this wing were ice cream parlors, Italian restaurants, pizza stands, donut shops, and many other *milchig* food concessions.

And, best of all, above both arrows was a sign announcing: We are diligent in our observance of *kashrus*. Please be careful not to bring dairy food to the meat side, and vice versa.

To Harriet, this was really something.

But as they continued on their way, little Shimon piped up with something which, to him, was even more impressive. "This mall is bigger and better than the Staten Island Mall — and there are even *mezuzot* on every doorway!"

He is right. There *is* something nice about living and raising one's children in a place where, in addition to houses, all hospitals and public buildings have *mezuzot* on their doorposts. In fact, here there is even a *law* that says that all government offices must have a kosher *mezuzah* on each doorframe!

Chanukah in the Air

I love the time of year when Chanukah is in the air. The feeling usually starts about a month beforehand, in the month of Cheshvan.

It's more than just the fact that every *makolet* and small outdoor *kiosk* [candy/newspaper stand] is selling *sufganyot* [the traditional Israeli, oil-drenched, jelly-filled donut, that is *only* available during the Chanukah season].

It's more than the fact that the store show-windows begin displaying menorahs and dreidels mixed in with the items that are for sale — from women's clothing to towels, to displays in hardware store windows. (I mean, till you've seen the display-window of a downtown shoe store filled with men's shoes, artfully mixed together with dreidels of all types and sizes, well, you just haven't seen a ready-for-Chanukah display window!)

It's even more than the newspaper ads for "Special Chanukah Sale of ..." or "In time for Chanukah...."

Or even the special menorah/dreidel artwork festooning all of the newspapers, magazines, and billboards weeks before the holiday.

It's the fact that the Chanukah holiday is unconsciously imprinted strongly everywhere you go and in everything you do.... And that it is so *natural* here.

For example, last Chanukah I spent some time in Haifa. And Haifa, you should know, is not a city renowned for its high level of Jewish observance.

I went into a supermarket because I needed to get something — and there, staring me in the face, were huge banners draped everywhere throughout the store, loudly proclaiming: With all purchases of over 200 shekels, you will receive, free of charge, two fresh *sufganyot*.

Not one. Two.

But to me, I guess the high point was when I bought a box of individually wrapped, chocolate-covered cookies. It was produced by a national Israeli firm, and had no markings on the outer wrapping that indicated anything special for Chanukah.

It was just a regular box of fancy cookies.

But I was in Israel.

And I bought it around Chanukah time.

And so when I opened up the box, there, nestled inside with the cookies, was a little dreidel.

Truly, only in Israel.

And at Purim...

It was three days before Purim, and Pnina, my newly married daughter, was accompanying her husband Ezriel B. to the local Health Care Clinic for some blood tests that he needed. Unpleasant, but what can you do? Yet being in Israel made it special....

The first thing to catch their eye, when walking into the main clinic, was a huge, gorgeous sign festooning the wall, announcing "HAPPY PURIM" in Hebrew. The tremendous poster was signed "Kupat Cholim Maccabi" — i.e., "Happy Purim" greetings from the entire national Maccabi Health Care Fund. Very

very nice.

And then, they noticed that all the usual signs which tell you where to stand and where to go to find the various offices, departments, services, etc., *all* of these signs were decorated with noise-makers, clowns, balloons, and other Purim pictures. Which really gave a Purim feeling to the entire building.

But then, on a large table in the waiting room, they noticed something which really made it impossible to doubt for a moment that Purim was truly approaching ... there, in the center of the table, was a very large basket filled to overflowing with small, plastic, brightly colored noise-makers — with another sign above announcing, "HAVE A HAPPY PURIM," and signed by the local Health Fund *workers*.

What a country!

On their way home after finishing the tests, Pnina and Ezriel stopped off at Photo Shwartz, a film store in the center of the city. There, on the counter for all the waiting customers, was a huge box of hamentashen with a sign announcing, "HELP YOURSELF."

The bank they went into next had stacks of brightly colored copies of Megillat Esther next to each bank teller for clients to take, and, as the two proceeded along the street, they passed a tremendous box of small holsters on the sidewalk in front of a clothing store — just the item needed for children dressing up in cowboy costumes. On the box was printed, in large letters, "FREE."

It was the days before Purim in Jerusalem.

Need a Ride?

My friend Sara W. had an interesting and somewhat unique experience a few days ago.

She had gone food-shopping for her week's groceries in a small supermarket that is approximately a 15-minute walk from her home.

As Sara, Baruch HaShem, has quite a large family, her purchases were more than enough to warrant a mishloach — a (sometimes free) home delivery of her groceries to her front door by the Sanhedria Supermarket.

Since Sara doesn't have a car, and since the weather was lovely and the double-carriage and four small children accompanying her made getting on a bus a little complicated, Sara opted for walking home. Her grocery order would follow later — but she anticipated being home in time for the delivery.

Five minutes into her walk home, Sara was startled to hear a truck-horn loudly honking and honking and honking.

As honking horns are somewhat unusual in Jerusalem, especially in residential neighborhoods, Sara looked around to see from whence came the noise.

Imagine Sara's surprise to see a truck across the street, with the driver's head stuck out of the window, and an arm wildly waving at her.

As soon as her attention had been caught, the truck driver leaped out of the truck and crossed the street to her.

Recognizing the man who works in the Sanhedria Supermarket, Sara was amazed to hear him offer her a ride

NEED A RIDE?

home, since he was delivering her order right then.

Amazement reached all bounds when, after agreeing and thanking him, the truck-driver immediately picked up her large double-carriage, and deposited it in the back of his truck.

Sara's four young children had a memorable truck ride home.

And Sara has a memory of a "simple" Jerusalem kindness that will last forever.

No Sales Pitch

Julie G. only came on aliyah two years ago.

So some things still surprise her.

In California, where she lived and started raising her family, all shopkeepers knew that, in order to succeed financially, one needed to encourage customers to purchase new products.

I mean, everyone understood that it is at least worthwhile to *try* to get someone to buy.

But then Julie came to Israel to live....

It all started when the beaters of her handmixer broke. She bought new ones, but, one day a few months later, while

NO SALES PITCH

making a cake, they locked.

Taking the entire handmixer to a neighborhood store which fixed as well as sold small electrical appliances, Julie was pleasantly surprised that the storeowner didn't try to sell her a new handmixer — even though hers was an old, American brand.

Commenting that she needed a new part, and that they weren't readily available in Israel for that brand of mixer, he suddenly stopped talking and looked up.

"You're in luck," he told Julie. "I remembered. I threw out a mixer of this same model just last night. Maybe it has the part you need. They haven't picked up the garbage yet."

And as Julie stood there open-mouthed, the man went out the door of his store, walked around to the garbage bin, and started searching inside it.

He found the broken mixer he had thrown out the night before, and spent a half hour trying to fix Julie's handmixer with this "replacement part."

Unfortunately, he was not successful. The teeth in this broken mixer also were not any good.

And, of course, since he hadn't fixed Julie's mixer, he didn't charge her anything for the attempt. Or for the time he had wasted. Or for the fact that he had scrounged around in a garbage bin looking to save her money.

And he didn't even pressure her to buy a new handmixer from his store.

Talk about learning from *kol adam* [every man]!

As Passover Approaches

From the moment Purim ends, the entire country of Israel switches gears. Newspaper ads speak of special Passover sales, cleaning products get particular prominence everywhere, and kosher-for-Pesach seals (under the supervision of at least one Rabbinic authority, though usually sporting at least two Rabbinic *hechsherim* for good measure) begin appearing on everything from aluminum foil and scouring powder, to household bleach. (Re: edible items, it is obvious, of course, that *hechsherim* in abundance appear on everything.)

Into the third week before Passover, display windows in all types of stores begin showing wine cups, four sons, and cardboard cutouts of round and square matzot.

Large chain supermarkets start the change-over with white shelf paper under kosher-for-Pesach canned goods. They usually seem to begin on the far right side of the supermarket, and you can tell how many weeks are left before Passover by the steady march of white-shelf-papered supermarket shelves moving left across the entire store, aisle by aisle. By four or five days before Passover, there isn't much besides the bread shelves that isn't kosher-for-Pesach in the Jerusalem food-stores.

Yes, you also know that Passover is getting closer by the conversation of women awaiting their turn on checkout lines. Complete strangers, with or without head-coverings, whether wearing skirts or even jeans, are busy comparing how far they've gotten in their cleaning, how many bedrooms they've finished, and if they've "started the kitchen" yet.

But how do you know that Pesach is only *days* away?

The municipality begins putting up small, metal bins around the city's neighborhoods.

These are special round, metal cans, attached to the ground with a short metal pole — with "*chametz*" stenciled in large Hebrew letters on the sides.

These "cans" are specifically intended for burning your *chametz* in.

And the idea was inaugurated while Jerusalem's city government was *not* particularly concerned with encouraging mitzvah observance.

Our Missing Soldier

Horror and tragedy can happen anywhere. We all know that.

The question is, how does everyone around you react to the tragedy.

When soldier Nachshon Mordechai Wachsman, z"l, was kidnapped several years ago by Arab terrorists, the whole country responded.

Politicians on Israel's extreme left, who had built entire political careers (and probably their lives, too) on trying to blur the differences between Jews and Arabs, suddenly said that "Arabs must recognize that all Jews are Nachshon Wachsman."

Friends of the Wachsman family immediately organized recitation of all the psalms in *Sefer Tehillim* daily, in neighborhoods throughout Jerusalem.

Community prayers at the Kotel, by both religious and "non-religious" Jews, was requested by the boy's father, in newspaper and radio interviews. (And Egged, Jerusalem's public bus service, added extra buses on the Kotel route for this purpose.)

The Chief Rabbi of Israel called on the entire populace of Israel to recite three particular *Tehillim* for Nachshon Mordechai Wachsman's safe return.

But though perhaps Jewish communities around the world would react to tragedy in much the same way, an 11:00 P.M. phone call from my friend Anna S. that same night highlighted the specialness of living in Israel, even during hard times.

Anna and her husband had just returned from doing their weekly grocery shopping, and she immediately called to let me know what an unbelievable thing she had just seen. (They came on aliyah six years ago, from New York.)

They had been shopping in the huge Jerusalem supermarket that was originally established by a Charedi political party for Yeshivah/*kollel* families.

And, as each and every customer paid for his purchases, he received, in addition to his change and the cash register receipt, a printed copy of the three Psalms with the name to be prayed for: Nachshon Mordechai ben Esther Gittel.

I'm not sure what impressed Anna more — the fact that the *Tehillim* sheets were prepared and being distributed only hours after the Chief Rabbi's call for *Tehillim* was publicized over the media, or the fact that, though this organization isn't particularly noted for following the dictates of the Chief Rabbinate, they did it anyway.

Perhaps what really astounded Anna most of all was the simple fact that a regular supermarket was handing out *Tehillim* sheets.

No Big Deal

Perhaps not every single life-in-Israel story will tug at your heart-strings or make your eyes fill with tears of pride. But that doesn't make it any the less impressive every time those nice little I-wish-I-could-tell-someone situations happen here in Israel.

Even if they're not earth-shattering.

Like the *mezuzot*.

I know Jewish homes everywhere in the world have *mezuzot* on their doorposts.

I also know that in Israel there are *mezuzot* on each and every doorframe in every hospital and public building throughout the Land. And, of course, all the hospitals and public buildings have a *mezuzah* not just on their outside doorframes, but on each and every internal office/hospital room doorpost as well.

Of course.

But how this effects our consciousness — that we *expect* there to be *mezuzot* on all doorframes — was brought home to me by a story recounted by a friend, who has a cousin from Russia who's been in Israel for twenty-three years.

This friend's cousin is not (yet) religious. She lives in Beersheva's secular environment, largely among people who aren't particularly known for their adherence to the laws of the Torah.

But, as with most of life in Israel, once you look past the surface, there are levels of *Yiddishkeit* and Jewishness infused into almost everybody and everything.

My friend told this Russian cousin about the tremendous new shopping mall in Jerusalem, and that she's never seen anything like it, even in America. And the best part of all, she continued, is the fact that it's Jewish — that there's even a *mezuzah* on each and every store and restaurant doorpost!

"What's so special about that?" this not-religious Russian cousin responded. "Of course there are *mezuzot* on all the doorframes. There's a *mezuzah* on every doorframe in every shopping center everywhere. Even our shopping center in Beersheva has *mezuzot* on all of the doorposts. Do you mean to say that in America they don't have *mezuzot* on shop doors?"

This woman, living in Israel for so many years, completely forgot that not all doorframes in the world sport *mezuzot*.

Now, this might seem to be a little thing, but it says a lot to me. In Israel, *mezuzot* on doorframes are so much a part of daily life, that one assumes it is like this everywhere.

But it's not.

It is definitely nice to always see a *mezuzah* on every doorpost that I walk by — no matter where in the country I happen to be. And it is nice that my children get used to seeing it, too.

But imagine what would be if I remembered to kiss each one with *kavanah*, remembering that HaShem is guarding us, as I entered and left every room!

What Can You Say?

Some young people in the Mevo Choron moshav started a small business selling freshly squeezed orange juice. The fresh juice is really delicious, has two *hechsherim*, and comes in gallon-sized plastic containers. Best of all, the juice is sold door to door, so I don't even have to leave the confines of my apartment.

There is one problem, however. I'm not always home when they come, sometime in the evening on Thursdays.

Last week I got lucky — on her way home from the grocery store, my young daughter saw the people while they were a few buildings away from ours, and she told them that we want their orange juice every week. She bought one gallon, but they wouldn't sell her a second until they were sure that they had enough for their other customers. So she gave them our address in case they had any extra juice to sell, and brought home the one gallon she had purchased.

That night we returned home late from a wedding. Imagine our surprise to see, next to our front door, another gallon container of fresh squeezed orange juice. Fantastic.

The very next morning I tried to contact them, to thank them for the extra orange juice, and to ask them where to send a check (and how much I owed them). But there was no phone number or address on the beautifully designed orange juice label. So I assumed that they didn't mind waiting an entire week to get paid.

I wrote myself a note that I owed them money for one gallon of orange juice, and waited until Thursday.

Except I soon realized that on that Thursday I had to go to a Bar Mitzvah.

As an organized person who was trained to always repay owed money immediately, I put fifty shekels into an envelope, and wrote the name of the company in large letters across the front as well as the words "for orange juice!" I also wrote, on the outside of the envelope, that I owed them for one orange juice from last week, and in addition requested that they please leave me another two orange juices this week, and let me know how much each one costs.

I taped this epistle onto my front door. Since many people come to our door each evening for *tzedakah*, and since I grew up in America, I didn't think it appropriate to add "Your money is in this evelope. Please leave me change." But, between the fact that I wrote on an envelope, and ordered additional orange juices besides the money I already owed them, and (I forgot to mention) I am a total stranger who has never seen any of them in my entire life, nor they, me...well, wouldn't you think a profit-making business would at least *try* to open the envelope in the hope of maybe getting the past money due them?!

But, only in Israel.... We returned from the Bar Mitzvah to find the two gallon containers of fresh squeezed orange juice next to the front door, and the envelope I had taped there with the price per container now written on it. My fifty-shekel bill was still inside. The people hadn't left me an accounting of how much I now owed them, nor did they write down their phone number or address so that I could make an accounting and send them the money. They just left the juice, and the price per container — not even restating that I owed them from the week before!

I mean, what can you say about a country where people give things to strangers trusting that they'll pay them some time in the future. And what can you say about a country where someone would leave anything for anybody in a public place, unguarded (just ask your friends who still live abroad) — especially when it is for strangers, and a matter of *parnasah*. I mean, what a country!